THE BIGGEST TONGUE TWISTER BOOK IN THE WORLD

Gyles Brandreth
Illustrations by Alex Chin

WINGS BOOKS
New York
Avenel, New Jersey

This 1992 edition is published by Wings Books,
distributed by Outlet Book Company,
a Random House Company, 40 Engelhard Avenue,
Avenel, New Jersey, 07001, by arrangement with
Sterling Publishing Company, Inc.

Printed and Bound in the United States of America

Library of Congress Cataloging-in-Publication Data

Brandreth, Gyles Daubeney, 1948–
    The biggest tongue twister book in the world / by Gyles Brandreth
; illustrations by Alex Chin.
        p.   cm.
    Originally published: New York : Sterling Pub Co., 1978.
    Summary: Pronouncing punishing puns provokes pure pleasure,
passing pain, plus palate paralysis with this comprehensive
collection of alphabetically arranged tongue twisters.
    ISBN 0-517-07768-X
    1. Tongue twisters.   [1. Tongue Twisters.]   I. Chin, Alex, ill.
II. Title.
[PN6371.5.B7   1992]
828′.91402—dc20   91-33303
                                                             CIP
                                                             AC

8 7 6 5 4 3 2 1

FOREWORD

If you are interested in tongue twisters—and if you have bought, borrowed or been given this book I certainly hope you are — you may have heard of Peter Piper, the well known picker of pecks of pickled peppers. The tongue twister about him (and you can read it in full on page 76) is probably the world's most famous tongue twister. It is the one I learned first. It is the one I like the best. And to be honest with you, until not so long ago it was the only one I really knew.

Some time ago I was hosting a radio show in which I gave each of the guest stars a different tongue twister and invited them to repeat it as many times as they could manage, without fumbling, faltering or having a fit, inside the space of 60 seconds. The star who managed to pack the most tongue twisters into his minute won a prize. It was a great game and my guests and I had a lot of fun with it. The listeners must have enjoyed it too because they began to send me their favorite tongue twisters. I could hardly believe my eyes when I read some of the ones people sent in and I could hardly believe my own ears when I heard myself trying to twist my tongue around them. Some were easy. Some were not so easy. Some were almost impossible and all of them you will find in the pages that follow.

I think it is fair to say that this book is the most comprehensive collection of tongue twisters ever published. It is not the first of course, but I like to think it is the best. The first — or, at least, one of the very first — was the slim volume in which Peter Piper first made an appearance in print. It was published in London in 1674 and was called *Peter Piper's Practical Principles of Plain and Perfect Pronunciation*. It contained just 24 tongue twisters, and I have reproduced each one of them at the very beginning of each of the chapters in this book. It also contained a delightful Preface and I cannot think of a better way of introducing you to the wonderful world of tangled tongues — tongled tangues, than by quoting it to you in full:

"Peter Piper, without Pretension to Precosity or Profoundness, Puts Pen to Paper to Produce these Puzzling Pages, Purposely to Please the Palates of Pretty Prattling Playfellows, Proudly Presuming that with Proper Penetration it will Probably, and Perhaps Positively, Prove a Peculiarly Pleasant and Profitable Path to Proper, Plain and Precise Pronunciation. He Prays Parents to Purchase this Playful Performance, Partly to Pay him for his Patience and Pains, Partly to Provide for the Profit of the Printers and Publishers, but Principally to Prevent the Pernicious Prevalence of Perverse Pronunciation."

GYLES BRANDRETH

Andrew Airpump asked his Aunt her ailment.
Did Andrew Airpump ask his Aunt her ailment?
If Andrew Airpump asked his Aunt her ailment,
Where was the ailment of Andrew Airpump's
Aunt?

Anthea and Andy ate acid apples accidentally.

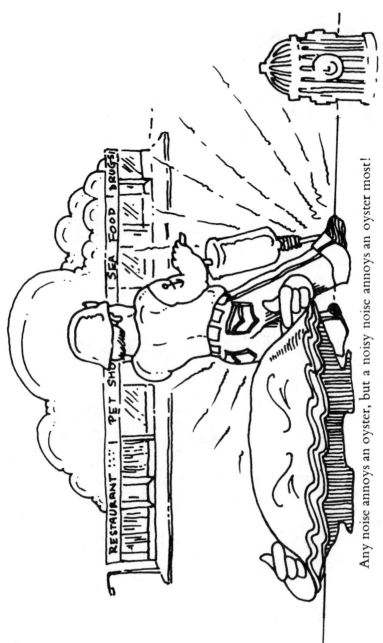

Any noise annoys an oyster, but a noisy noise annoys an oyster most!

Am I and Amy aiming anemic anemones on my many
enemies?

I'm anti Auntie!

Amidst the mists and coldest frosts,
  With barest wrists and stoutest boasts
He thrusts his fists against the posts,
  But still insists he sees the ghosts.

Asking Arthur Askey.

When all else fails, say 'Hail to all males!'

Antidisestablishmentarianism.

The apples fermented inside the lamented
  And made cider inside her inside!

Billy Button bought a buttered biscuit.
Did Billy Button buy a buttered biscuit?
If Billy Button bought a buttered biscuit,
Where's the buttered biscuit Billy Button bought?

Blame the big bleak black book.

You sent me your bill, Berry,
Before it was due, Berry;
Your father, the elder Berry,
Isn't such a goose, Berry.

Boiled beef and broad beans.

A black-backed bath brush.

Rubber baby-buggy
bumpers.

Black bugs' blood.

The big
black-backed
bumblebee.

Once upon a barren moor
   There dwelt a bear, also a boar.
The bear could not bear the boar,
   The boar thought the bear a bore.
At last the bear could bear no more
   That boar that bored him on the moor.
And so one morn he bored the boar —
   That boar will bore the bear no more!

Bill Badger brought the bear
a bit of boiled bacon in a
brown bag.

Billy's big blue badly-bleeding blister.

The bleak breeze blights the bright blue blossom.

Betty Block brought back black bric-a-brac.

Bring back the "Brighton Belle"!

Broad-beamed Bertha breathes bad breath.

Good blood, bad blood.

I go by Blue Goose bus.

Bright blue blisters bleeding badly.

I brought the blazer braid I bought to bind the blazer blue.
The braid I bought was not too bright to bind the blazer
blue.

The beet that beat the beet that beat the other beet is now beaten by a beet that beats all the beets, whether the original beet that beat the beet or the beet that beat the beet that beat the other beet!

Big brown bumblebees were buried beside the bulbs in Bobby Brook's bulb bowls, baskets and boxes.

Bill had a billboard,
Bill also had a board bill,
The board bill bored Bill,
So Bill sold the billboard
To pay his board bill.
The board bill no longer bored Bill.

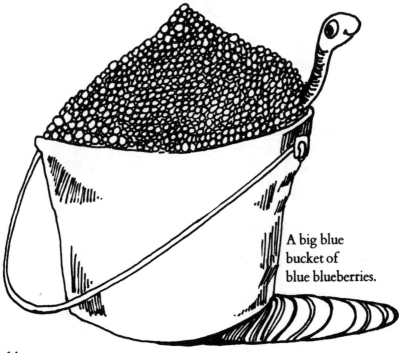

A big blue
bucket of
blue blueberries.

Betty Botter
  bought some butter.
"But," she said,
  "the butter's bitter.
If I put it
  in my batter,
It will make
  my batter bitter.
But a bit
  of better butter —
That would make
  my batter better."

So she bought
  a bit of butter,
Better than
  her bitter butter.
And she put it
  in her batter,
And the batter
  was not bitter.
So 'twas better
  Betty Botter
Bought a bit
  of better butter!

Little Boy Blue
a big blue bubble blew.

The busy bee buzzed busily
around the busy beehive.

15

Black dog danced
on the barn floor barefoot.

Bright blows the broom on the brook's bare brown banks.

Betty beat a bit of butter to make a better batter.

"The bun is better buttered," Billy muttered.

Billy Button buttoned his bright brown boots and blue
coat before breakfast began.

Beautiful babbling brooks bubble between blossoming banks.

Beautiful Bonnie Bliss blows blissfully beautiful bubbles.

Babbling Bert blamed Bess.

The bootblack brought the boot back.

The brisk, brave brigadiers brandished broad bright blades, blunderbusses and bludgeons.

Barbara burned the brown bread badly.

Three blue beads in a blue bladder rattle blue beads, rattle blue bladder.

The bottom of the butter bucket is the buttered bucket bottom.

Thad Blake's back brake-block broke.

A bootblack blacks boots with a black blacking-brush.

The broom blooms when the bluebells bloom.

Bulb-bowls.

Betty Blue
blows big black bubbles.

The big baker
bakes black bread.

The best blowing bugler in the Boston brass band.

Captain Crackskull cracked a catchpoll's
   cockscomb.
Did Captain Crackskull catch a catchpoll's
   cockscomb?
If Captain Crackskull cracked a catchpoll's
   cockscomb,
Where's the catchpoll's cockscomb Captain
   Crackskull cracked?

The cat-catchers
can't catch
caught cats.

This crisp crust crackles crunchily.

We eat what we can
and what we can't we can.

The crime completed, the coward crawled cautiously
coastward.

Father Coward's crack crazed the crowded congregation.

The cox crew rowed at cock's crow.

How many cuckoos could a good cook cook if a good cook
could cook cuckoos?

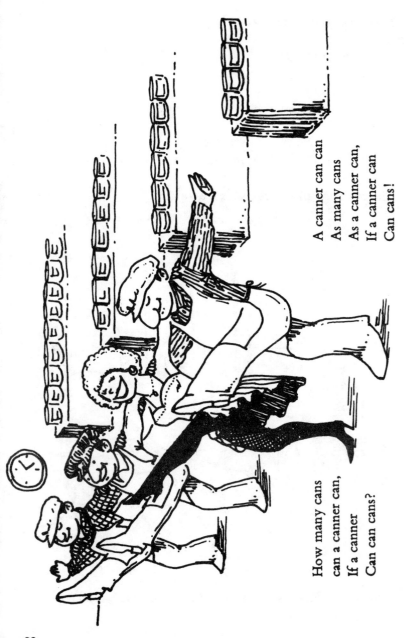

How many cans
can a canner can,
If a canner
Can can cans?

A canner can can
As many cans
As a canner can,
If a canner can
Can cans!

Cook cooked a cup of cold creamy custard.

A cricket critic cricked his neck at a critical cricket match.

Cheryl's chilly cheap chips shop sells Cheryl's cheap chips.

Great crates create great craters.

Clearly the clause in Klaus's contract causes Klaus confusion.

Mrs. Cripp's cat crept into the crypt, crept round and crept out through a crack.

A laurel-crowned clown.

Catch
a can canner
canning a can
as he does the can-can
and
you've caught
a
can-canning
can-canning
can canner!

Can a canner can-can?

Cross-eyed Clara's
Crazy over crosswords,
She's got competitions on the brain.
When she's working, everybody's weary,
She's wrapped up in her dictionary.
Ma's cross, Pa's cross,
Everybody's got cross ways,
And it's quite imposs
To avoid getting cross
With cross-eyed Clara and her crossword craze.

Cross crossings cautiously!

A crow flew over the river with a lump of raw liver.

The fish-and-chips shop's chips are soft chips.

"Cheep-cheep," chirped the cheery chaffinch.

Cheerful children chant charming tunes.

Cameron came careering round the corner, completing his
crazy career by crashing into the crypt.

If a good cook could cook cuckoos so fine
And a good cook could cook cuckoos all the time,
How many cuckoos could a good cook cook
If a good cook could cook cuckoos?

Crazy Clara catches crawling crabs.

Cuthbert was caught coughing in his coffin.

The crazy cockroach crowned the crooked cricket.

All I want is a proper cup of coffee
Made in a proper copper coffee pot.
You can believe it or not,
But I just want a cup of coffee
In a proper coffee pot.
Tin coffee pots
Or iron coffee pots
Are no use to me.
If I can't have
A proper cup of coffee
In a proper copper coffee pot,
I'll have a cup of tea!

A clipper ship shipped several clipped sheep.
Were these clipped sheep the clipper ship's sheep?
Or just clipped sheep shipped on a clipper's ship!

Cliff Cross crossed the criss-cross crossing.
The criss-cross crossing Cliff Cross crossed.
When Cliff Cross crossed the criss-cross crossing,
Where's the criss-cross crossing Cliff Cross crossed?

Can Kitty cuddle Katie's kitten?

Crime cuts cut crime.

A canner exceedingly canny,
One day remarked to his granny:
"A canner can can
Anything that he can,
But a canner can't can a can, can he?"

How much caramel can a canny cannibal cram into a
camel, if a canny cannibal can cram caramel into a camel?

Charlie chooses
cheese and cherries.

Davy Dolldrum dreamed he drove a dragon.
Did Davy Dolldrum dream he drove a dragon?
If Davy Dolldrum dreamed he drove a dragon,
Where's the dragon Davy Dolldrum dreamed he
drove?

The drain in the train dripped again and again
Until the drain in the train dripped dry!

If a dog chews shoes, what shoes should he choose to chew?

Deeply dreadful dreams.

Did you do it? Don't do it!

A dozen double damask dinner napkins.

Do drop in at the Dewdrop Inn.

The dude designed the desperate plot to dupe the dreadful desperado.

The Duke dragged the dizzy Dane down into the deep damp dank dungeon.

Dimpled Dina danced in a dainty dimity down the dunes.

Dashing Daniel defied David to deliver Dora from the dawning danger.

Diligence dismisseth despondency.

Daring Dan dashed dizzily down the dale doing damaging deeds as he went.

If one doctor doctors another doctor, does the doctor who doctors the doctor doctor the doctor the way the doctor he is doctoring doctors? Or does he doctor the doctor the way the doctor who doctors doctors?

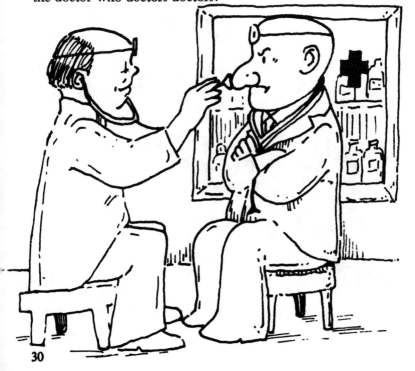

Double bubble gum
bubbles double.

The dim don dropped the drum.

Dressed in drip-dry drawers.

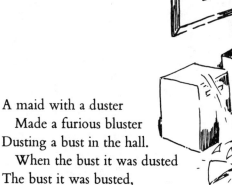

A maid with a duster
    Made a furious bluster
Dusting a bust in the hall.
    When the bust it was dusted
The bust it was busted,
    The bust it was dust, that's all.

Enoch Elkrig ate an empty eggshell.
Did Enoch Elkrig eat an empty eggshell?
If Enoch Elkrig ate an empty eggshell,
Where's the empty eggshell Enoch Elkrig ate?

Eleven elves in Hell.

Eli eats eels from Ealing.

And ere the ear had heard,
Her heart had heard.

"Aye! Aye!" said the Ear.
"Hear! Hear!" said the Eye.

Even Stephen's even oven's on.

Last year I could not hear
with either ear.

Evel Knievel helped himself to eleven lots of elevenses.

An elevator on Everest: on Everest an elevator.

Even Evan's eaten eighteen eggs.

Elevating eleven elephants.

Even the hare's hair
hides the hare's ears.

Francis Fribble figured on a Frenchman's filly.
Did Francis Fribble figure on a Frenchman's filly?
If Francis Fribble figured on a Frenchman's filly,
Where's the Frenchman's filly Francis
    Fribble figured on?

Four fat friars frying flat fish.

Frightened Philip forced fearful Frank to fence furiously.

Francis Fowler's father fried five floundering flounders for
Francis Fowler's father's father.

For fine fresh fish phone Phil.

A lively young fisher named Fischer
  Fished for fish from the edge of a fissure.
A fish with a grin
  Pulled the fisherman in!
Now they're fishing the fissure
  For Fischer!

A fat-thighed freak fries thick fish.

Five French friars fanning a faint flea.

Fetch fifty-five foils.

Flee from fog to fight flu fast!

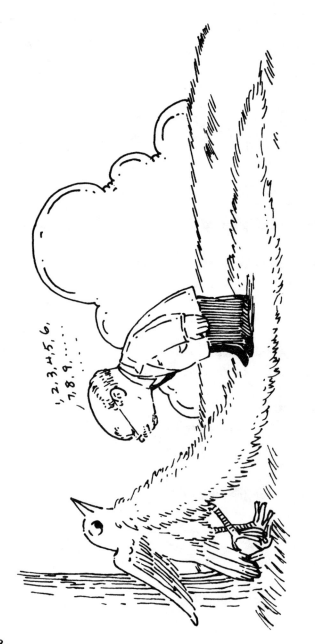

There are thirty thousand feathers on that thrush's throat.

Said the flea to the fly as he flew through the flue,
"There's a flaw in the floor of the flue."
Said the fly to the flea as he flew through the flue,
"A flaw in the floor of the flue doesn't bother me.
Does it bother you?"

Freddy thrush flies through thick fog!

Frisky Freddie feeds on fresh fried fish.

Five fashionable females flying to France for fresh French
fashions.

Fresh fried flesh of fowl.

Flora's fan fluttered feebly and her fine fingers fidgeted.

Figs form fine fancy fare.

Four famished French fishermen frying flying fish.

Forty fat farmers found a field of fine fresh fodder.
Now, if forty fat farmers found a field of fine fresh fodder,
Where is the field of fine fresh fodder those forty fat farmers
found?

Five frantic fat frogs fled from fifty fierce fishes.

Three free flow pipes.

Three fluffy feathers fell from Phoebe's feeble fan.

Fancy Nancy didn't fancy doing fancy work. But Fancy
Nancy's fancy aunty did fancy Fancy Nancy doing fancy work!

Four fat dogs frying fritters and fiddling ferociously.

A fine field of wheat. A field of fine wheat.

Frightened fluffy owls flying foolishly through the farmyard.

Francis fries fish fillets for Frederick. Frederick fillets four
fresh fish for Francis's fried fillets.

Of all the felt I ever felt
I never felt a piece of felt
That felt the same as that felt felt,
When I first felt that felt.

Five flashy flappers
Flitting forth fleetly
Found four flightly flappers
Flirting flippantly.

Pure food for famished
pure mules.

A fly flew past Flo's flat,
And a fly flew past fat Flo.
Is the fly that flew past Flo
The same fly that flew past fat Flo's flat?

Ted threw Fred three free throws.

The first fast master passed faster than the last just pastor.

There was an old lady called Farr,
Who took the 3:03 for Forfar.
She said, "I believe
It's sure to leave
Before the 4:04 for Forfar!"

Threadbare Fred feeds on fried fresh fish, fish fried fresh,
fresh fried fish, fresh fish fried and fish fresh fried, does
threadbare Fred.

Four famous fishermen found four flounders — flippers
flapping furiously! — faithfully following four floppy female
flat-fish.

Freckled-faced Florence.

Fancy Fanny Franks feeling funny about Fred Ferraby's
fishing flies, for Fred Ferraby fishes with flies to catch frisky
fishes.

41

Gaffer Gilpin grabbed a goose and gander.
Did Gaffer Gilpin grab a goose and gander?
If Gaffer Gilpin grabbed a goose and gander,
Where are the goose and gander Gaffer Gilpin
grabbed?

Georgia's George
is gorgeous.

Gertrude Gray gazed at the gray goose gaily.

Green greengages grow in green greengage trees.

"Goodbye, Gertie," gushed Gussie.
"Goodbye Gussie," gushed Gertie.

Our great-grand-gran is a greater great-grand-gran than your great-grand-gran is.

Give George green gloves and gleaming galoshes.

Gay Gladys glanced bravely at grave Greta and glided glitteringly past guilty Grace at the glorious garden gala.

Groovy gravy, baby!

George Gabs grabs crabs,
Crabs George Gabs grabs.
If George Gabs grabs crabs,
Where are the crabs
George Gabs grabs?

Gig-whip.
Gig-whip.
Gig-whip.

Good, better, best.
Never let it rest,
Till your good is better
And your better best.

Cows graze in droves on grass which grows in grooves on groves.

Grace's gray-green gloves glided gracefully to the ground.

The cruel ghoul's cool gruel.

Gaily gathered the gleaners
the glossy golden grain
and garnered it gladly
in Granny's great granary
in Godfrey's green glassy glen.

"Good Morning, Madam,"
To Eve said Adam.
"Good Morning, Sir,"
To him said Madam.

A Glasgow glazier's gloriously gleaming green glass
gas-globes.

The gum glue
grew glum.

Eight gray geese gazing gaily into Greece.

Three gray geese crept into Clitheroe Castle. Out of Clitheroe Castle crept three gray geese.

The glow-worm's gleam glitters in glade and glen.

The grave gamesman groused when the greyhound growled.

He generally reads regularly in a government library particularly rich in Coptic manuscripts except during the month of February.

A glowing gleam glowing green.

Granny's gray goose greedily gobbled golden grain in Graham's gabled granary.

Gregory Grimes groaned with a grim grimace.

Gaze on the gray gay brigade.

Gloria Groot glued a groat to Gregory's goat.

Greek grapes.

Humphrey Hunchback had a hundred hedgehogs.
Did Humphrey Hunchback have a hundred hedgehogs?
If Humphrey Hunchback had a hundred hedgehogs
Where are the hundred hedgehogs Humphrey
Hunchback had?

A haddock!
A haddock!
A black-spotted haddock!
A black spot
On the black back
Of a black-spotted haddock!

Hungry Harry's
homely uncle.

The horses' hard hoofs hit the hard high road.

One hundred air-inhaling elephants.

The hares' ears heard ere the hares heeded.

Bees hoard heaps of honey in hives.

If to hoot and to toot
  A Hottentot tot,
Was taught by a Hottentot tutor.
  Should the tutor get hot,
If the Hottentot tot
  Hoots and toots
At the Hottentot tutor?

The hedge hindered
the homicidal hombre
from hurting himself.

How high His Highness holds his haughty head!

If a Hottentot taught
    A Hottentot tot,
To talk ere the tot could totter,
    Ought the Hottentot tot
Be taught to say 'ought,'
    Or what ought to be taught her?

Houston has hosts of huge houses and heaps of high horses.

The heir's hair gets into the heir's ear.

If a hair net could net hair,
How much hair
Could that hair net net,
If that hair net could net hair?

Has Helen heard how Hilda hurried home?

He bade him eat his own hot ham, so his own hot ham he ate.

Hath Hazel asthma?

His hat hit Horace, so Horace hollered horribly.

Hams hung up. Hung up hams.

Albert had a habit of eating hot halibut.

"Hold him here!" hollered Harold.

Heather was hoping to hop to Tahiti
To hack a hibiscus to hang on her hat.
Now Heather has hundreds of hats on her hat rack,
So how can a hop to Tahiti help that?

It ain't the hunting on the hills that hurts the horses' hoofs.
It's the hammer, hammer, hammer on the high road home.

Oh, Horace!
Isn't it horrible when you're hot and in a hurry,
And you've got to hold your hat in your hand?!

I often sit and think
and fish and sit
and fish and think
and sit and fish
and think and wish
that I could get a cool drink!

He ran from the Indies
to the Andes
in his undies!

If a chicken and a half laid an egg and a half in a day and a
half, the farmer wouldn't have a fit and a half!

I thought a thought.
But the thought I thought wasn't the thought I thought I
    thought.
If the thought I thought I thought had been the thought
    I thought, I wouldn't have thought so much.

It is better to ride in a car and think it is better to ride in a
car than it is to walk and think it is better to ride in a car
than it is to walk.

Where ignorance predominates, vulgarity invariably asserts itself.

"I can think of thin things, six thin things, can you?"
"Yes, I can think of six thin things, and of six thick things, too."

I shot three shy thrushes. You shoot three shy thrushes.

I do like cheap sea trips,
Cheap sea trips on ships.
I like to be on the deep blue sea,
When the ship she rolls and dips.

I wished I hadn't washed this wrist watch.
I've washed all the wheels and works.
Oh, how it jumps and jerks.
I wish I hadn't washed this watch's works!

Can you imagine,
an imaginary menagerie manager
imagining managing an imaginary menagerie?

I was looking back
To see if she was looking back
To see if I was looking back
To see if she was looking back at me.

Jumping Jackey jeered a jesting juggler.
Did Jumping Jackey jeer a jesting juggler?
If Jumping Jackey jeered a jesting juggler,
Where's the jesting juggler Jumping Jackey jeered?

A jester from Leicester
Went to see Esther,
But as Esther was taking her siesta,
The jester from Leicester didn't see Esther.

Joan joyously joined jaunty John in jiggling jugs.

Jean, Joan, George and Gerald judged generally.

Jingling George jiggled juice in a jar.

Juvenile Jack Jones jumped jerkily on Jimmy in the gymnasium.

James just jostled Jean.

Our Joe wants to know if your Joe will lend our Joe your Joe's banjo. If your Joe won't lend our Joe your Joe's banjo our Joe won't lend your Joe our Joe's banjo when our Joe has a banjo!

Kimbo Kemble kicked his kinsman's kettle.
Did Kimbo Kemble kick his kinsman's kettle?
If Kimbo Kemble kicked his kinsman's kettle,
Where's the kinsman's kettle Kimbo Kemble kicked?

Can King Kong kiss quicker than Queen Kate?

A kiss is the anatomical juxtaposition of two orbicularis oris muscles in a state of contraction.

Cute Kate's knitting knotted nighties for the Navy.

I saw Esau kissing Kate.
I saw Esau. He saw me.
And she saw I saw Esau.

Nina needs nine knitting needles to knit naughty Nita's knickers nicely.

Knott was not in.
Knott was out
Knotting knots in netting.
Knott was out,
But lots of knots
Were in Knott's knotty netting.

Can Kitty cuddle
Clara's kitten?

Mr. Knox
Keeps his socks
In a pale pink chocolate box.
They're orange socks
With spots
And clocks.

Kiss her quickly!
Kiss her quicker!

A knapsack strap.

Quick kiss!
Quicker kiss!
Quickest kiss!

Lanky Lawrence lost his lass and lobster.
Did Lanky Lawrence lose his lass and lobster?
If Lanky Lawrence lost his lass and lobster,
Where are the lass and lobster Lanky Lawrence lost?

Lovely lilacs line Lee's lonely lane.

Lucy lingered, looking longingly for her lost lapdog.

Look at the bug tug at the rug!

Leila listened to the lilt of the lark.

Elizabeth lisps lengthy lessons.

Don't run along the wrong lane!

A lump of red leather.
A red leather lump.

Red leather!
Yellow leather!

High roller.
Low roller.
Lower a roller.

A library littered with literary literature.

Lesser leather never weathered lesser wetter weather.

The lone lovers leave the leafy lane.

Let us go together to gather lettuce, whether the weather will let us or no.

There is a layer of bones in the lion's lair.

Lots of little London lamp-lighters lit London's lot of little lamps.

The bad lad limps gladly along the badly-lighted landing.

Listen listlessly to the lilting lullabies.

The liar says he can play the lyre.

Lame lambs limp.

This lute, with its flute-like tones, was captured in the loot of a great city, and its luminous sides are made of unpolluted silver.

Lottie licks lollies lolling in the lobby.

Lemon liniment.

A woman in a plaid shawl shoveled soft snow slowly.

He is literally literary.

A tall eastern girl named Short long loved a big Mr. Little. But Little, thinking little of Short, loved a little lass named Long. To belittle Long, Short announced she would marry Little before long. This caused Little shortly to marry Long. To make a long story short, did tall Short love big Little less because Little loved little Long more?

Matthew Mendlegs missed a meddling monkey.
Did Matthew Mendlegs miss a meddling monkey?
If Matthew Mendlegs missed a meddling monkey,
Where's the meddling monkey Matthew Mendlegs
missed?

My Miss Smith lisps and lists. She lisps as she talks and she
lists as she walks.

Mr., Mrs., Master and Miss Moth meet Miss, Master, Mrs. and
Mr. Moss.

My mother made Mary, Minnie and Molly march many
times around the room to martial music.

Too many merry moments make mad Madge mischievous.

My dame hath a lame tame crane.
　My dame hath a crane that is lame.
Pray, gentle Jane, let my dame's tame crane
　Feed and come home again.

"Are you copper-bottoming 'em, my man?"
"No, I'm aluminuming 'em, Ma'am!"

"Mortals may not match my magic," muttered the magician
menacingly.

Mr. Maston must miss his mascot the mastiff.

Many an anemone sees an enemy anemone.

Many million minis merrily milling mid minstrels.

Mixed metaphors muddle middling minds.

The mighty master murdered the maddened magistrate.

The minx mixed a medicinal mixture.

Many mincing maidens meandered moodily moonwards.

A monk's monkey mounted a monastery wall munching
mashed melon and melted macaroni.

Messy May Messant may,
but musing Maisie May mustn't.

A maid in Waltham, mum,
Once played the National Anthem, mum.
And broke a chrysanthemum, mum.

Mr. Matthew Mathers munches mashed marmalade muffins.

The musician made music and moved multitudes.

'Manners maketh man,' mouthed Mick.

My master said that that "that" is the right "that" in that
particular place.

Miss Maggie MacGregor makes magnificent macaroons.

Mumbling bumblings. Bumbling mumblings.

The other mother's smothered in moss.

This myth is a mystery to me.

The myth of Miss Muffet.

There's the Mayor's mayoral mule.

Neddie Noodle nipped his neighbour's nutmegs.
Did Neddie Noodle nip his neighbour's nutmegs?
If Neddie Noodle nipped his neighbour's nutmegs,
Where are the neighbour's nutmegs Neddie Noodle nipped?

"Night, night, Knight," said one Knight to the other Knight
the other night. "Night, night, Knight."

"Have you got the knack of the new knapsack strap, Nat?"

Ninety-nine naughty knitted nick-nacks were nicked by
ninety-nine naughty, naughty knitted nick-nack nickers.

Now nine nice nurses need necklaces.

Nine nestlings nestle nightly in their nine nests.

Nifty Nina nibbles nice knobbly nougat.

Ned needed to name no new names.

Ned Nott was shot
  and Sam Shott was not.
So it is better to be Shott
  than Nott.
Some say Nott
  was not shot.
But Shott says
  he shot Nott.
Either the shot Shott shot
  at Nott
Was not shot,
  or Nott was shot.
If the shot Shott shot
  shot Nott
Nott was shot,
  but if the shot Shott shot
shot Shott
  Then Shott was shot not Nott.
However, the shot Shott shot
  shot not Shott, but Nott.

Nine naughty nanny-goats nibbled nine nice new
nasturtiums.

I need not your needles, they're needless to me,
For needing needles were needless you see.
But did my neat trousers but need to be kneed,
I then should have need of your needles indeed.

Nice nieces nestle nicely in Nice.

Nine nimble noblemen nibble nuts.

The new nuns knew the true nuns knew the new nuns too.

Oliver Oglethorpe ogled an owl and oyster.
Did Oliver Oglethorpe ogle an owl and oyster?
If Oliver Oglethorpe ogled an owl and oyster,
Where are the owl and oyster Oliver Oglethorpe
    ogled?

> Oh! that I was where I would be,
> Then would I be where I am not.
> But where I am there I must be,
> And where I would be, I cannot.

Angelina oiled the hinges on her oil engine with oil-engine oil.

Our black bull bled black blood.

One old owl
occupies one old oak.

An oyster met an oyster,
  And they were oysters two;
Two oysters met two oysters.
  And they were oysters too;
Four oysters met a pint of milk,
  And they were oyster stew!

Oporto, a port in Portugal, exports port.

Tiny orangutan tongues.

Old oily Ollie oils oily autos.

The owner of the Inside Inn
Was outside his Inside Inn,
With his inside outside his Inside Inn.

Peter Piper picked a peck of pickled peppers.
Did Peter Piper pick a peck of pickled peppers?
If Peter Piper picked a peck of pickled peppers,
Where's the peck of pickled peppers Peter Piper
picked?

Pink silk socks with shot silk spots.

The poor dog's paw poured water from every pore.

Pragmatic politicians pontificate precociously.

Pretty posies prancing proudly.

Plain bun, plum bun, bun without plum.

A purely rural duel truly plural is better than a purely plural duel truly rural.

Tom brought some fine prime pink popcorn from the prime pink popcorn shop.

Pretty Polly Perkin polished paper plates and plaster plaques.

Proud Percival pestered the pilgrim for the promised prayer.

The Pope poked a poker at the piper,
so the piper poked some pepper at the Pope!

Mrs. Pipple Popple popped a pebble in poor Polly Pepper's eye.

A bearded peer on the pier appeared to peer in the pier glass.

Peter Payntor the painter prefers painting pink pigs to picking pretty purple pansies.

A pale pink proud peacock pompously preened its pretty plumage.

Plain plump Pansy played picquet pleasantly.

Please, Paul, pause for applause.

Peter Palmer painted a paper peacock, purple, pink and puce.

Penelope Pringle printed press paragraphs.

Peppercorn pudding and pelican pie.

The praising princess picked a pretty pleasing posy.

Put the cut pumpkin in a pipkin.

Pete's Pa, Pete, popped off to the pea patch to pick a peck of peas for the poor pink pig in the big pig pen.

Is there a pleasant peasant present?

A pleasant place to place plates is a place where the plates are pleased to be placed.

A poor pauper paused on purpose to pawn a porpoise.

Quixote Quicksight quizzed a queerish quidbox.
Did Quixote Quicksight quiz a queerish quidbox?
If Quixote Quicksight quizzed a queerish quidbox,
Where's the queerish quidbox Quixote Quicksight
quizzed?

Quin's twin sisters sing tongue twisters.

The new King's queen.
The new Queen's king.

Curious quiet calm.

A queer quick questioning quiz.

Quick quiet quills quote Quinney's quarrel.

Quick — Quack — Quock
Quack — Quock — Quick
Quock — Quick — Quack

Quick, whitewash wicked quicksand quite white.

The quaint queen quickly quelled the quarrelsome Quaker!

Rory Rumpus rode a rawboned racer.
Did Rory Rumpus ride a rawboned racer?
If Rory Rumpus rode a rawboned racer,
Where's the rawboned racer Rory Rumpus rode?

Rich Rajahs ride reindeers with red rope reins around their
regal necks.

Robin Redbreast's bad breath.

As the roaring rocket rose,
the restless roosters rollicked.

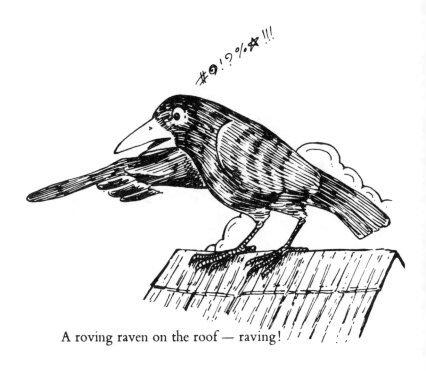

A roving raven on the roof — raving!

The rat ran by the river with a lump of raw liver.

Richard gave Robert a rap in the ribs for roasting his rabbit so rare.

Rush the washing, Russell!

The religious relic reposed in the reliquary.

A regal rural ruler.

I can't stand rotten writing when it's written rotten.

The wire wound around a reel.

Round and round the rugged rocks the ragged rascal ran.

Real roses rustle rurally.

Rupert wrestled rashly with Robin.

Red rubies, round ring.

Rascally ruffians robbed the Regent.

The Regent was rightly regally royal in his rightly regally royal regalia!

Miss Ruth's red roof.

Rita relishes Russian radishes.

If Roland Reynolds rolled a round roll around a round room, where is the round roll which Roland Reynolds rolled around the room?

Reds rule. Blue rules.

Reading bells ring rapidly and reeds rustle around rivers.

Roads close, so snow slows shows.

The royal lady received the roses regally at the recent reception.

The red wretched bull put his foot in the bucket.

Sammy Smellie smelt a smell of small-coal.
Did Sammy Smellie smell a smell of small-coal?
If Sammy Smellie smelt a smell of small-coal,
Where's the smell of small-coal Sammy Smellie
smelt?

On the beach I saw six small seals.

The savor of the silly scent the sentry sent to Millicent.

Slapped slimy slush shivers slightly.

Simon Squirrel sold Swiss sweets and shapeless sheep
swathed in Shetland shawls.

Shy sly Sheila sat shivering in her slim, shiny silk smock.

Swedish sword swallowers shift short swords swiftly.

She says she shall sew a sheet.

If neither he sells seashells,
Nor she sells seashells,
Who shall sell seashells?
Shall seashells be sold?

The strenuous struggle strangles the strong.

The strapping soldiers strived sternly to strengthen the stronghold.

We surely shall see the sun shine soon.

When does the wristwatch strap shop shut?
Does the wristwatch strap shop shut soon?
Which wristwatch straps are Swiss wristwatch straps?

Six southern sailors sailing southern seas.

I snuff shop snuff.
Do you snuff shop snuff?

Six shivering sailors swam steadily shoreward.

Seventy shuddering sailors stood silent as short sharp shattering shocks shook the splendid ship.

Six skyscrapers stood snugly side by side, shimmering by the seashore.

Sixty-six shy schoolmasters sailing serenely a ship on a shining sea.

The sunshade sheltered Sarah from the sunshine.

Does this shop stock
short socks with spots?

She stood at the threshold of Mrs. Smith's fish shop
welcoming him in.

The sun shines on shop signs.

Flocking shoppers stopping and shopping.

Sally's selfish selling shellfish,
So Sally's shellfish seldom sell.

Mr. See owned a saw
  And Mr. Soar owned a seesaw.
Now See's saw sawed Soar's seesaw
  Before Soar saw See,
Which made Soar sore.
  Had Soar seen See's saw
Before See sawed Soar's seesaw,
  See's saw would not have sawed
Soar's seesaw.
  So See's saw sawed Soar's seesaw.
But it was sad to see Soar so sore
  Just because See's saw sawed
Soar's seesaw!

Mr. Spock spoke softly
of specific space specifications.

Six thick thistle sticks.

Which switch, miss, is the right switch for Ipswich?

A sick sparrow sang six sad Spring songs sitting sheltering under a squat shrub.

Six Silician snakes sibilantly sang six silly serenades to six Serbian serpents.

Sheila's Shetland pony shied,
Shooting Sheila on the shore.
Shaking Sheila, stupefied,
Struggled homeward, stiff and sore.

A shy little she said "Shoo!"
To a fly and a flea in a flue.

Soldiers' shoulders shudder when shrill shells shriek.

Shears have sharp shining points.

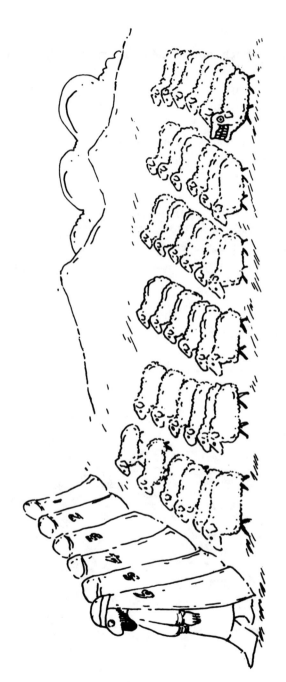

The sixth sheik's sixth sheep's sick!

Sheep shouldn't sleep in a shack.
Sheep should sleep in a shed.

Susan Schumann shot a solitary chamois and received a short, sharp salutary shock from such shameless slaughter.

"Sheath thy sword," the surly sheriff said, "or surely shall a churlish serf soon shatter thee."

If a shipshape ship shop stocks six shipshape shop-soiled ships,
How many shipshape shop-soiled ships would six shipshape ship shops stock?

Suppose Sally shredded suet so swiftly that she was sooner done than she expected,
How slowly would Sally have to shred suet to be done as soon as she expected she would be?

The shepherds share the Shetland shawl.

Please sell me some short silk socks and some shimmering satin sashes.

Stop chop shops selling chopped shop chops.

Some say sweet-scented shaving soap soothes sore skins.

She is a thistle sifter
and she has a sieve of sifted thistles,
and a sieve of unsifted thistles,
and the sieve of unsifted thistles
she sieves into the sieve of sifted thistles,
because she is a thistle sifter.

Through six thick swamps stumbled Sammy.

A shifty snake selling snakeskin slippers.

As I was going past Mr. Young's yard,
I saw a man sawing.
And of all the saws I ever saw,
I never saw a saw saw like that saw sawed!

Sister Suzie's sewing shirts for soldiers.
Some skill at sewing shirts our shy young Suzie shows.
Some soldiers sent epistles
Saying they'd sooner sleep on thistles
Than miss the saucy soft short shirts for soldiers
Sister Suzie sews.

The short sort shoot straight through.

Snow slight: no snipe.

Saucy Sally saw Silly Sam sowing sunflower seeds.
If Silly Sam saw Saucy Sally seeing him sow sunflower
    seeds,
Should Silly Sam sob?

With a shovel Sarah slowly shifted sifted cinders.

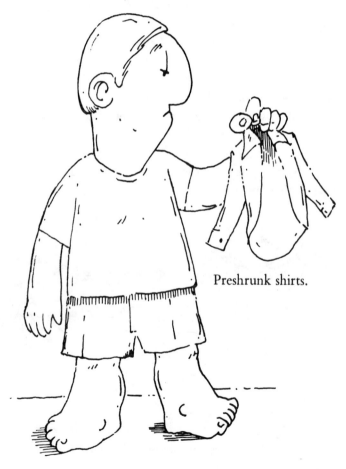

Preshrunk shirts.

Swim, Sam, swim,
Show them you're a swimmer!
Six sharp sharks seek small snacks,
So swim, Sam, swim!

Now a sleeping car's known as a sleeper,
And sleepers for sleepers they keep,
And sleepers run under the sleepers
In which those sleepy sleepers sleep.

If a top were to sleep in a sleeper,
And the sleeper beneath him went pop,
It's a logical cert that the top would get hurt,
For there's no sleeper that sleeps like a top!

Slim Sam slid sideways.

His shirt soon shrank in the suds.

Mrs. Snelling's selling six sick shorn sheep.

She sells seashells on the seashore, but *she* sells seashells, sherry and sandshoes on the seashore.

Strange strategic statistics.

Of all the smells I have ever smelt,
I never smelt a smell
that smelt like that smell smelt.

Solemn Sam slammed the door.

A shooting suit that's suitable for shooting,
Should be made of a suiting that is suitable.
If not made of a suiting that is suitable,
Then that shooting suit's not suitable for shooting!

The sinking steamer sank!

Sarah saw a sash shop full of showy, shiny sashes.

Shipshape suit shops ship shapely suits.

Shoes and socks shock Suzie.

Shy Sheila shakes soft shimmering silks.

A ship saileth south soon.

She sewed shirts seriously.

Six short soldiers sang a short song while scrubbing six
short shirts sister Suzie sewed.

Six silly sisters sell silk to six sickly seniors.

Shave a cedar shingle thin.

A single solid silver sifter sifts sifted sugar.

Down the slippery slide they slid
Sitting slightly sideways;
Slipping swiftly see them skid
On holidays and Fridays.

The swan swims!
The swan swam!
The swimming swan swam on the sea!

Sooty Sukey shook some soot from sister Suzie's sooty shoes.

Swan, swim over the sea.
Swim, swan, swim!
Swan, swim back again.
Well swum, swan!

She saw thirty-four swift sloops swing shorewards before she saw forty-three spaceships soar.

Slim satellites sending scintillating signals.

Strikes strangle struggle, squandering scheduled synthesis.

Students study stencilling steadily.

Sammy sitting singing
Sought Suzie Shaw.
Since Suzie's started sobbing,
Sammy's stopped seeking.

Meet Sir Cecil Thistlethwaite, the celebrated theological
statistician.

Softly, silently the scythe
Slithered through the thick sweet sward:
Seething, sweating, sad serfs writhe,
Slicing swaths so straight and broad.

If a sleeper in a sleeper sleeps,
does the sleeper not in the sleeper on the sleeper sleep?

I miss my Swiss Miss. My Swiss Miss misses me.

Sue said she should show the shrewd shrew the same shoe she
threw the shrewd shrew.

Say this sharply, say this sweetly,
Say this shortly, say this softly,
Say this sixteen times in succession.

She stops at the shops where I shop,
and if she shops at the shop where I shop
I won't stop at the shop where she shops!

Shirley slid the scissors down the slippery slanting slats.

Shy Sam Smith thought Sarah Short so sweet.

Susan shineth shoes and socks,
Socks and shoes shineth Susan.
She ceaseth shining shoes and socks,
For socks and shoes shock Susan.

Slim Sam shaved six slippery chins in sixty-six seconds.

Silly Sammy Stokes spilt some sticky syrup on the stove.

The saucy slippery scoundrel scampered scurrying by.

The subtle scent of the supple sweet honeysuckle is
satisfying to savor.

The seething sea ceaseth, and thus the seething sea
sufficeth us.

She saw the shiny soap suds sailing down the shallow sink.

Sister Suzie sneezes slightly,
Slicing succulent shallots.

A skunk sat on a stump.
The skunk thunk the stump stunk,
And the stump thunk the skunk stunk.

Tiptoe Tommy turned a Turk for twopence.
Did Tiptoe Tommy turn a Turk for twopence?
If Tiptoe Tommy turned a Turk for twopence,
Where's the Turk for twopence Tiptoe Tommy
turned?

Then the thankless theologian
thawed thoroughly.

I buy my suits from Theophilus Thistlethwaite, the tailor at thirty-three South Twelfth Street.

A thin little boy picked six thick thistle sticks.

On two thousand acres, too tangled for tilling,
Where thousands of thorn trees grew thrifty and thrilling,
Theophilus Twistle, less thrifty than some,
Thrust three thousand thistles through the thick of his thumb!

A tidy tiger tied a tie tighter to tidy her tiny tail.

They tried to tempt the tattered tramps to take the toothsome tarts.

Typical tropical trivial trite trash.

The truants tramp trustingly towards Troy.

107

Tonight is a light night,
So you mustn't light a night light,
On a light night like this.

When a twiner a twisting will twist him a twist,
For the twining his twist he three times doth entwist,
But if one of the twines of the twist do untwist,
The twine that untwisteth, untwisteth the twist.

Untwirling the twine that untwisteth between,
He twists with his twister the twain in a twine;
Then twice having twisted the twines of the twine,
He twisteth the twines he had twisted in vain.

The twain that, in twisting before in the twine,
As twines were entwisted, he now doth untwine,
'Twixt the twain intertwisting a twine more between,
He, twisting his twister, makes a twist of the twine.

Tiny Tom toddles to
the tiny toddlers'
toyshop.

Tom turned to Ted,
Told Ted to try
To tie the tie
Tom tried to tie.

Thelma saw thistles in the thick thatch.

A tooter who tooted a flute
   Tried to tutor two tutors to toot.
Said the two to their tutor,
   "Is it harder to toot or
To tutor two tutors to toot?"

Thrice times three.
Twice times two.

The two-twenty tore through town.

Toy boat.

Miss MacIntyre's tiresome tire on her tricycle twisted.

Of all the ties
I ever tied,
I never tied a tie
Like this tie ties.

Twelve typical typological typographers typically translating the typography of topical, tropical typographical types!

Twine twisted twigs twenty twirls.

Through thicket and bush the thirty thirsty Thracians thrust.

> A tree toad loved a she-toad
>   That lived up in a tree.
> She was a three-toed tree toad,
>   But a two-toed toad was he.
> The two-toed toad tried to win
>   The she-toad's friendly nod,
> For the two-toed toad loved the ground
>   On which the three-toed toad trod,
> But no matter how the two-toed tree toad tried,
>   He could not please her whim.
> In her tree-toad bower,
>   With her three-toed power,
> The she-toad vetoed him.

Three thumping tigers tickling trout.

Ten thatchers went to thatch ten tiny thatched cottages, taking ten tight bundles of thatching straw with them to thatch with.

Three sick thrushes sang thirty-six thrilling songs.

Ten tongue-tied tailors twisted tinted thistles with their teeth.
If ten tongue-tied tailors twisted tinted thistles with their teeth,
Who tinted the tinted thistles that the ten tongue-tied tailors twisted?

They threw three thick things.

Three thrushes thrilled them.

Two thirsty thatchers thoughtfully thatched a thrush's
nest – such a thankless task!

They thanked them thoroughly.

Three Scotch thistles in the thicket.

Ten tame tadpoles tucked tightly together in a thin tall tin.

Tuesday is stew day.
Stew day is Tuesday.

A twister of twists
    Once twisted a twist,
And the twist that he twisted
    Was a three-twisted twist.
Now in twisting this twist,
    If a twist should untwist,
The twist that untwisted
    Would untwist the twist.

Ten tiny toddling tots trying to train their tongues to trill.

Twenty talented teachers teaching tiny tots their two times table.

Twenty tinkers took two hundred tin tacks to Toy Town.
If twenty tinkers took two hundred tin tacks to Toy Town,
How many tin tacks to Toy Town did each of the
twenty tinkers going to Toy Town take?

The twenty-to-two train to Tooting tootled tunefully as it tore through the tunnel.

Tommy Tickle tickled his teacher. Where did Tommy Tickle's teacher tickle Tommy?

The tiresome wireless man's fireless,
Whilst the fireless wireless man's tireless.

Thus the thug threatened the thoroughly thoughtful theologian.

Thin sticks; thick bricks.

Three thrice-freed thieves.

Do breath tests test the breath?
Yes, that's the best of a breath test.
So the best breath stands the breath test best!

Three thick black plastic press blocks as previously supplied.

The tracker tracked and tricked and trapped the tricky trickster.

Send ten tons of pink-tinted toilet tissue to Tom Timms.

Timothy took Titus to Tavistock to teach the tomtits to talk theology to the Turks that travel through Tartary.

The threaded beads thrilled them.

If Timothy Theophilus Thicklethwaite Thwackum thrust
his two thick thumbs through three hundred and
thirty-three thousand three hundred and thirty-three thick
and thin thistles, where are the three hundred and
thirty-three thousand three hundred and thirty-three thick
and thin thistles that Timothy Theophilus Thicklethwaite
Thwackum thrust his two thick thumbs through?

Timothy Taylor twiddled tightly twisted twine ten times to
test it.

Two tubby turtles toasting tasty tea-cakes.

Tom threw Tim three thumbtacks.

The troops tread the toilsome trail.

Twelve tall tulips turning to the sun.

Uncle's Usher urged an ugly urchin.
Did Uncle's Usher urge an ugly urchin?
If Uncle's Usher urged an ugly urchin,
Where's the ugly urchin Uncle's Usher urged?

Handy Andy's got his Sunday undies on!

Unique New York.

United States twin-screw steel cruisers.

Once I heard a mother utter,
"Daughter, go and shut the shutter."
"Shutter's shut," the daughter uttered,
"For I can't shut it any shutter."

Uncle Eric's irksome ulcer.

Urgent detergent.

The host in Ulster uttered an oath.
What was the oath the Ulster host uttered?

Unless the two tots titter,
You'll tell the oft-told tale.

You mustn't mutter matter, you must utter it.

Villiam Veedom viped his vig and vaistcoat.
Did Villiam Veedom vipe his vig and vaistcoat?
If Villiam Veedom viped his vig and vaistcoat,
Where are the vig and vaistcoat Villiam Veedom
viped?

Vera Van Vostock waited while Walter Van Winkle wooed
in vain.

One violet winkle veering west via Worthing went wading
round Ventor.

Vigorous Vesta voiced voluble verse vociferously.

Violet vainly viewed the vast, vacant vista.

Virile Victor vanquished vain vendors.

Vile Willy's wily violin.

Vera valued the valley violets.

Valiant vassals vexed Victoria.

Vim. Van. Van. Vim.

Walter Waddle won a walking wager.
Did Walter Waddle win a walking wager?
If Walter Waddle won a walking wager,
Where's the walking wager Walter Waddle won?

Little Willie's wooden whistle wouldn't whistle.

Wheedling, weeping Winnie wails wildly.

Wood said he would carry the wood through the wood.
And if Wood said he would, Wood would.

Thirty thrifty whistling washers witchingly whistling,
wishing washing was washed.

My wife gave Mr. Snipe's wife's knife a wipe.

Whistle for the thistle sifter.

Who washed Washington's white woolen underwear, when
Washington's washerwoman went west?

Which is the witch that wished the wicked wish?

The wild wind whipped Will White from the wharf.

Wishy-washy Wilfrid wished to win a wager.

Which witch had the wen on her hand when we met them, and you asked them whether we should have fine weather?

Weak writers want white ruled writing paper.

Will real wheels really wheel?

Wise wives whistle while weaving worsted waistcoats.

Esau Wood sawed wood. Esau Wood would saw wood. Oh, the wood that Wood would saw! One day Esau Wood saw a saw saw wood as no other woodsaw Wood ever saw would saw wood. Of all the woodsaws Wood ever saw saw wood, Wood never saw a woodsaw that would saw wood like the woodsaw Wood saw would saw wood. Now Esau Wood saws with that saw he saw saw wood.

I wonder whither the weather will waft the wherry wherein the weather is, and whether the wherry will weather the weather.

Oswald Whittle's whistle outwhistles all other whistlers' whistles in Oswaldtwistle.

A white witch watched a woebegone walrus winding white wool.

The wild wolf roams the wintry wastes.

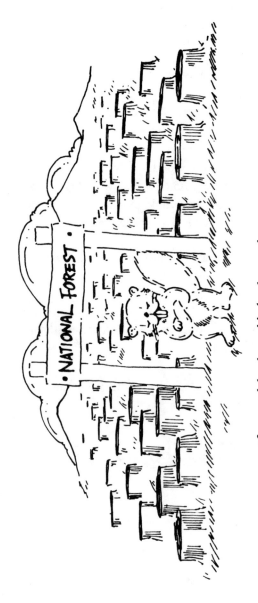

If a woodchuck could chuck wood,
how much wood would a woodchuck chuck
if a woodchuck could chuck wood?
He would chuck, he would,
as much as he could,
if a woodchuck could chuck wood.